A MIND

PRAIRIE SCHOONER BOOK PRIZE IN POETRY | EDITOR **KWAME DAWES**

LIKE THIS

Susan Blackwell Ramsey

To you —
Master of the villanelle!
Susan

UNIVERSITY OF NEBRASKA PRESS | LINCOLN AND LONDON

Acknowledgments for the use of
copyrighted material appear on
pages xii–xiii, which constitute an
extension of the copyright page.

Library of Congress
Cataloging-in-Publication Data
Ramsey, Susan Blackwell.
A mind like this / Susan
Blackwell Ramsey.
p. cm. — (Prairie Schooner
Book Prize in Poetry)
Poems.
ISBN 978-0-8032-4338-5
(pbk.: alk. paper)
I. Title.
PS3618.A4785M56 2012
811'.6—dc23
2012004732

Set in Granjon by Bob Reitz.
Designed by Nathan Putens.

For Dorothy Blackwell, who taught me to read.
Thanks to you I've always felt safe.

And for Wayne Ramsey, my luckiest break—
and the only person in the world who reads
poetry but doesn't write it.

Which of you is literary, and
which one likes to dance?

NICHOLAS DELBANCO
What Remains

CONTENTS

SOURCE ACKNOWLEDGMENTS

The Atlanta Review: "Children in Church"

CALYX: "Stalling," "Why I Hate Storytellers" (as "Storytellers")

The Hiram Review: "I'm in Love with Leonard Woolf," "Consider Hairs"

The Indiana Review: "Tell Me If You've Heard This One"

Margie: The American Journal of Poetry: "Lidian Emerson Watches Her House Burn, Concord, July 23, 1872"

Marlboro Review: "The Genome for Luck," "Sexing the Alligator"

New Poems from the Third Coast: An Anthology of Michigan Poets [Wayne State University Press, 2000]: "Aftereffects of Bell's Palsy," "Our Third Wedding Reception This Year Hits Its Stride"

Passages North: "Lilium Orientale"

Poetry East: "Amplification," "And All Trades, Their Gear and Tackle and Trim," "Gaudeamus, Full Band Version," "Pattern and Ground"

Poetry Northwest: "Emerson's Eyes," "Letter to Matt on the Opening Day of Deer Season," "A Mind Like This," "Outside Interests," "To a Picky Eater at Love's Table," "Washing My Husband's Kilt Hose: A 32-Bar Reel"

Prairie Schooner: "Peripheral: Emerson, 1847," "Pickled Heads: St. Petersburg"

Primavera: "Aftereffects of Bell's Palsy"

Rhino: "Mariah Educates the Sensitive," "Louise Erdrich Learning Ojibiwemowin"

River Styx: "The Year Hits Perimenopause"

Southern Poetry Review: "The Comfort of Pickup Trucks" (as "Hometown Funerals"), "In Order to Swallow, a Frog Has to Close Its Eyes,"

Southern Review: "Boliche," "Elegy from Halfway Up the Drive," "January Tulips," "Mount St. Helen's, May 18, 1980," "Neruda in Kalamazoo"
Tar River: "Stalling"

"Lidian Emerson Watches Her House Burn, Concord, July 23, 1872" won the 2007 Marjorie J. Wilson award from *Margie: The American Journal of Poetry*.
"Pickled Heads: St. Petersburg" was chosen by David Wagoner for *Best American Poetry 2009*.

With thanks to ~
    Gail Martin, my first, best reader
The teachers ~
in Kalamazoo: Conrad Hilberry, Diane Seuss, John Rybicki, David Dodd Lee, Scott Bade
at Notre Dame: Cornelius Eady, Joyelle McSweeney, Orlando Menes, Nuala Ni Dhomhnaill, Valerie Sayers (and Coleen Hoover for making it all work)
The Sunday Group: Kit Almy, Marion Boyer, Danna Ephland, Conrad Hilberry, Gail Martin, Christine Horton
Dawgs, in all its ever-changing forms
Martha Silano, volcano of daring
    Judy Myers, Betsy Ramsey Bird, Ben Ramsey, and Kate Ramsey, prime movers

A MIND LIKE THIS

PICKLED HEADS: ST. PETERSBURG

For years they floated in adjacent jars,
    two heads on a dusty storage shelf,
abandoned in a back room of the palace:
    Mary Hamilton and Charles Mons.

We want to make things last. Salt, sugar, sun
    will work, and tannin from chestnut bark, and brains
spread on the skins that toted them, and sometimes
    words. But new two hundred years ago —

these "spirits of wine." (Fermenting's nature, but
    distilling's art.) Not all steam is water,
just as not all passion's love. Boil wine,
    catch what evaporates, trap that alcohol

and it preserves whatever you drop in,
    the head of your wife's lover, for example —
Peter ordered his queen to display it on her mantle —
    or your mistress, killed for infanticide.

They say Great Peter kissed the dead head's lips.
    The bodies sinned, the heads were saved. Don't be
distracted by stories of Joaquín Murrieta
    glaring in a jar in California.

Though he was gunned down by someone named Love,
    his problems were political, not erotic.
He really should remind you of Evita,
    beautifully embalmed, better than Lenin,

then passed around, hot political potato,
    hidden in attics, propped like a doll behind
a movie screen for weeks, deaths unfurling behind her
    like a red scarf from Isadora's car.

And even if Jeremy Bentham's head was found
    once in a luggage locker in Aberdeen,
once in the front quadrangle being used
    as a football by medical students, he died

a natural death and landed in that cabinet,
    stuffed, propped, dressed through his own will,
wax head on his shoulders, catastrophe in the drawer,
    still convinced Utility was his goal.

The uses the dead are put to by the living.
    Peter saved one for hatred, one for love,
and they outlasted hatred, love, and Peter
    to become flip sides of Death's two-headed coin.

Heads win. Maybe the story
    isn't the heads but Peter, unstoppable
monster consuming youth, a Minotaur
    trapped in the labyrinth he built himself.

Finally Catherine freed them. After decades
    she found them, observed how well their youth and beauty
were preserved, and had them buried, though no one says
    whether bottled or free to stop being beautiful.

LOUISE ERDRICH LEARNING OJIBIWEMOWIN

Two-thirds of Ojibiwemowin is verbs,
    and nouns aren't male and female, they're living or dead.
(She's learning the language so she'll get the jokes.)
    The word for stone, *asin*, is animate.

If nouns aren't male and female, but living or dead,
    what you think you know begins to shift.
Their word for stone, asin, is animate
    and that universe came from a conversation of stones.

Of course what you know will have to shift
    since every language has its limitations.
What's geology but a conversation of stones?
    and even we know flint does speak to steel.

But every language has its limitations:
    French doesn't really have a word for warm,
flint will only speak its sparks to steel,
    there's no word for privacy in Chinese.

French has only *tiede*, which means lukewarm.
    Can you have a concept without the word?
Certainly there's no privacy in China.
    So English added chutzpah, macho, chic,

until we grasped the concept, owned the word
    by borrowing it so long it felt like ours,
which takes chutzpah. Macho is learned, and chic
    can't be taught, but both take a straight face—

borrow one until it feels like yours.
    It's useful, too, for poker, tango, jokes,
all teachable skills improved by a straight face,
    by knowing what will concentrate your power.

What improves your poem, tango, jokes—
    she's learning the language so she'll get the jokes—
is knowing what will concentrate your power:
    two-thirds of Ojibewemowin is verbs.

TELL ME IF YOU'VE HEARD THIS ONE

Surprise is what we value in a joke
we think, a different reason for the chicken
to cross, a deeper basement to the blonde's
bemusement, some new group screwing in a lightbulb,
odder animal walks into a bar,
the final wise word from the patient rabbi.

A priest, a Baptist minister, and a rabbi
walk into a bar. Barkeep says "Is this a joke?"
Sure, and a good one, a world where every bar
is just as apt to host a talking chicken
as an ecumenical conference, but no lightbulb
ever flashing on above the blonde.

It's compensation, making fun of blondes,
just like giving the punchline to the rabbi.
The proud are humbled, the oppressed triumph, the lightbulb
goes on — we get it, and laugh. A joke
turns power upside down until a chicken
can be the hero and walk into a bar.

And everyone seems welcome here, bar
none, not just the always-welcome blonde
but those who'd be justified in feeling chicken
about walking in, the solitary rabbi

stranded amid goyim who wouldn't get the jokes
he tells at home, grateful that these lightbulbs

are dim. You'd have to be a pretty dim bulb
not to know that everyone in this bar
has been the butt of the lowest kind of joke,
history's hotfoot, fate's yanked-out chair. Blondes
took over one dark night and riddled the Polacks, the rabbi,
Cletus hazed Rastus, but yo' mama fried that chicken

so good everybody was happy, even the chicken.
It's verbal potluck: Luigi brings a bulb
of garlic, knock-knock the drummer delivers pizza, the rabbi
adds a little schmaltz, everyone in the bar
is flaunting their roots, eventually even the blonde.
The melting pot's a plate, a glass, a joke.

"Rabbi, how many moths to screw in a lightbulb?"
asks the blonde chick at bar. "Only two." "No joke?"
"But like us, you've got to wonder how they got in there."

KALAMAZOO DECIDES SHE LIKES HER NAME

It's true she used to cringe when people laughed.
    She'd wish she had a normal name, like Springfield,
but the way Glen Miller savored her name
    letter by letter helped, it really did.
She started to feel special, briefly drew
    those O's as double hearts, then razor-trimmed it
to an edgy "'Zoo."
        Kalamazoo.
           She says it slowly, rolls it
on her tongue, over the pebbles in feeder creeks,
    the *a*'s flat as Midwestern prairies, the *z*
buzzing in wild lupines, that single *l*
    bobbing back and forth between the *a*'s,
meadowlark on a grass stem, the final *oo*
    waist deep in that long grass, glad
at having tricked your lips into a kiss.

"AND ALL TRADES, THEIR GEAR AND TACKLE AND TRIM"

Hopkins got it right, the way the mind
delights in shop talk, jargon. Love of craft
becomes a love of tools and words for tools
and words for skills in using tools, the haft
or maiden, cullet, shaft or frass or frit.

The great saw blade goes dishy ripping oak. Flaws
in your Sunday color supplement are called
hickeys, and cursing pressmen know they're caused
by specks that they remove with hickey-pickers.
Adobe sells "alternate ligatures and glyphs."

This need to differentiate, this passion
for precision peeled your hand out of a paw
just as using it in a three-jawed chuck
or five-jawed cradle grip slowly changed the brain
learning to fashion tools from stick, rocks, words.

So farmers have farriers, barrows, farrowings,
harrows, creep-feeders, teasers, drenches, gilts,
and some of us, hearing scumbling discussed,
listen harder to artists, finding our reward
in Strathmore four-ply plate-finish Bristol board.

BOLICHE

All through high school Paul's nickname was Boliche
    because in seventh grade Spanish class he bragged
"Yo soy más boliche!" which translates to
    "I am more bowling!" It made a certain sense

when you remember the fad in language teaching
    for immersion: conversation, vocabulary,
but never grammar, never a hint that Spanish
    was a different building, not just repainted English;

so if the book said that "I like bowling better"
    in Spanish goes, *"Me gusta más el boliche,"*
then *boliche* must mean "better." We had to learn
    that no one ever likes anything in Spanish;

things are pleasing to you, a small stone wall
    we tripped over, and getting up looked back
at our own house, yard, from a different angle.
    It was a first attempt to fit our thinking

in another's, like empathy or ballroom dancing.
    It felt perverse, a deliberate obstacle,
like the Swiss building railroads a smaller gauge
    than every other country's to thwart invasion,

which forced us to wake and reluctantly stumble
    across the border lugging packs and passports,
to walk fifty feet, climb on, and start again,
    learning new words just so they could give us grades.

I hope old Boliche got an A.
    While the rest of us slumped in language lab,
going through the motions, lockstepping our way
    from one unconsidered language to another,

Boliche grabbed a flag, wrapped it around his neck,
    ran off into the trees, picked a bowling ball,
and took a big bite. Of course he got it wrong,
    but he got it wrong the right way. When I skip

tourist attractions because they're a cliché,
    don't dance when Los Bandits are playing in the park,
decline to sing along, every time I blink
    instead of winking, wear black instead of red,

I'm back in language lab, back in junior high,
    for which the translation is *purgatorio*,
but a place for learning, where learning may get you out,
    out, and if you're lucky, *más boliche*.

PERIPHERAL: EMERSON, 1847

Bill says I'm right, he learned it in the service —
    night vision is different. You have to train your eyes

to one side of what you want to see. It works
    for faint stars, too. Orion's testicles

blink on, blink off, like the neon martini
    over some rundown bar. Let focus go,

and the secrets moving through the long blades of grass
    change from point to wave, to pattern, plot.

To draw a chair, draw the spaces between the legs.
    Paint only shadows — your brain supplies the face.

The bodies were gone by the time they found Pompeii,
    but ash shaped casts around what once was there,

as peripheral people may define the shape
    of someone otherwise too big to see.

(Andrew Wyeth painted his father as a hill.)
    So don't focus on this house where turnpike

meets Great Country Road. Try glancing east
    where gawkers watch Alcott hammer that summerhouse

Emerson's kindness commissioned — nine posts, not from need
    but for the Muses, and nearly more nails than lumber,

or focus on this coach delivering
    Aunt Mary Moody Emerson, four foot two,

traveling with her coffin, wearing her shroud,
    whose letters shaped his brain. Or come out back

and climb up on this branch with me. Right now
    apples are Emerson's passion. We'll peer between

leaves the way pinhole and paper
    let you watch eclipse and not go blind.

His boy's been buried these five years. In March
    he pruned every tree to let in light — the rule

is to trim everything that grows up or in
    and a third of everything that's left.

    *

Lace is by nature peripheral but may
be saved, passed on, after the garment frays.

The unicorn tapestries were used as tarps
in fields and orchards for a hundred years.

Tapestry weavers must work from the back.
Lace is a regular pattern of absences.

KNITTING LACE

Like any widow, any amputee,
    lace is defined by absence,
by what is missing, lack.
    There is no such thing
        as solid lace.

It's possible
    to churn out lace by rote,
each row executed, crossed off, mere
    mechanics of fingers, thread.
        But lace craves

full engagement, the moment
    that you grasp
its particular logic, spot
    the error in the row below, know
        how to fix it,

not ripping out whole rows,
    but dropping down
one stitch, amending, climbing back up
    to go on waltzing, stitch, space, stitch,
counting with the body, not the brain.

Lace makes you concentrate.
     No coasting, cruising,
mind in neutral, fingers ticking off
     a rosary of repetitious stitches.
          Lace takes

your best attention,
     the park bench in your brain
where math and language hunch
     over a chessboard, leaves blowing
          past their ankles.

THE DUC DE SAINT-SIMON BUYS
LADY MURASAKI A DRINK

from The Bistros of Heaven and Hell

He examines the ceramic sake cup.
She moves the fan to her left hand to grasp
the slender crystal stem. She understands
him to say that, like her incense mixtures,
this wine blooms for those attuned to nuance.
They smile. Nuance is oxygen to them.

However much their formal costumes differ —
and from lowered lids she eyes his lace,
while he in turn approves her multiple cuffs:
green, three graded pinks, three layered whites,
the sequence known as "Under the Snow"—they share
a bedrock of assumptions. They know Court.

They really are well bred, for even as
the alcohol takes hold and she forgets
her fan, she still won't stare, she never giggles
at his huge wig made of hair that curls.
He orders champagne, hoping to make her laugh,
not suspecting how carefully true ladies black their teeth.

JANUARY, TULIPS

Wheat would not outlast man seven years,
sheep are bred past shedding and must be sheared.
Peasent pleasures — honey, sunflowers, drums —
evolve to Mozart, crème brûlée, these tulips.
Some flowers look their best with furniture.

We plant them badly, martial blocks and squadrons,
spread swathes of them as if they were mere pigment.
And they don't help. Blown bald by normal winds,
snapped by passing dogs, prostrate in rain.

Outside, they're rigid, stiff. Inside, among
all these right angles, they are composed of curve.
On a lamplit table at eye level, color
humbles us. They're solid flames: gas blue
bases, orange petals feathered yellow
where the rims seems to flicker in the draft,
saved from the natural to be themselves.

GAUDEAMUS, FULL BAND VERSION

Eric Clapton's "Layla" is a mess
I love, wailing guitar lament refuted
by rich piano, the guitars relenting
in the end but no real resolution,
just a dwindling, a musical entropy,
like a toddler slipping from tantrum into sleep.

I'm a musical moron who would rather play
Bach in the background while I brush my teeth
than sit with a symphony orchestra, missing my knitting.
So why do I tear up every time I hear
that high note in the final line of Brahms's
"Academic Festival Overture"?

It is, after all, a glorious joke,
response to being told a thank-you postcard
in exchange for an honorary doctorate
is insufficient. Very well, Brahms responded,
and sent that ponderous title to them, scored
for the biggest orchestra of his life.

Size matters. I downloaded a favorite song
and thought I'd been wrong to like it, felt memory
had gilded it, or that age had drained the pleasure,
like ears or tongue dulling, until my son suggested

"You've got 'Acoustic.' Try the 'Full Band Version.'"
Brahms himself never went to college, but when

he was twenty he spent one glorious summer
living in Gröttingen with a friend who did.
Everything looks better from outside,
golden in lamplight. Brahms was no academic,
but he remembered those passionate bullshit sessions,
the arguments, the laughter, and the songs.

Especially the songs. So he chose a format,
formal, intricate, interweaving themes
and variations—but those themes are drinking songs.
The faculty begins to twitch and fidget.
The kids grin, then begin to sing along.
Young Clapton began with climax and worked backward;

Brahms, being old, knew how to postpone pleasure
until, strings running up and down like squirrels,
permitting himself cymbals, the brass grabs you
by the hair and slams you on your feet
singing, whether you know the words or not,
"Gaudeamus Igatur," "While we are young,

let us rejoice." Let the faculty fume,
their egos cheated of glory. Let Clapton pluck
an unplugged tribute to his own lost youth.
Old Brahms blows out the back wall with the joy
of being young, then tops it with that note,
that smile concealed behind the big gray beard.

A MIND LIKE THIS

is like looking through that drawer
for Scotch tape and coming up instead
with the instructions for the digital watch
you threw away three years ago, a maze
made of cheap pink plastic and three ball bearings,
the scissors you warned them were only for fabric, a roll
of the paper tape they gave you to close your eye
for sleep that spring you had Bell's Palsy, and half
a pack of basil seeds.

It's missing the Big Play because you're busy watching
the lovers' quarrel two rows down, look up
as the crowd surges to its feet around you,
touchdown. It's knowing they used sets from *King Kong*
as tinder for the burning of Atlanta
while being uncertain of your best friend's birthday,
forgetting the name of your fifth niece, but knowing Carlo
was Emily Dickinson's dog. When a mind like this
hears that Burleigh Grimes was the last pitcher
to throw a legal spitball in '43,
you'd think it had spotted a sapphire in the gravel.
It's saving pocket lint and bottle caps
while bread and diamonds thunder down the chute.

It's a theater where pleasure and frustration
are mutual understudies, a computer
that refuses to interface seven-fifteenths of the time.
It's dutifully viewing the list of cathedral features
in Strasbourg, then watching the memories dragged like sand
from a beach besieged by wave after wave of years,
until only a bit of carved stone remains, a fragment
small enough to lodge in a human heart.
Of course you didn't take a photograph.
And of course sensible friends return with cameras
full of statues and windows and twenty-foot clocks,
asking vaguely, "Where was that again?"
Be comforted. This ridiculous mind will save
your incised memory of the tenth pulpit step,
preserving for you how some particular hand
carved under a stone leaf, small in all that grandeur,
his round-skulled puppy, sleeping, chin on paws.

THE COMFORT OF PICKUP TRUCKS

I want warriors at my funeral,
each red-necked, milk-chested fellow
in his one tie, a suit that used to fit.
They make great pallbearers,
are okay at the grave, in any role
where silence is required, but it's hard
to get them inside afterward,
church basement, at the house. They clump
in the parking lot, out in the yard,
near the comfort of pickup trucks. While the women
chat and fuss, put out sandwiches, potato salad,
despair-black coffee, the men
talk in short words, call the dead man
by his last name, his clan. In the second hour
the laughter starts. They're stepping back,
as they used to from the pyre they'd pile
with axes, spears, gold rings,
away from that heat changing flesh to story.

WHY I HATE STORYTELLERS

Professional storytellers creep me out,
their vests and ribbons, long skirts, picturesque hats,
their shouts and whispers, hands fluttering like bats,
relentless eye contact staring me into squirm.

They're the Siegfrieds, Roys of story, cracking whips,
forcing sullen stories to sit up,
briefly paw air, snarling as they leap
through rings of fire, landing on heavy paws.

Good stories sneak up, they're glimpsed, overheard
from the booth behind you at the diner,
from the back seat, six hours into the trip,
on the radio, half over when you tune in.

Real storytellers are quiet, even reluctant.
Casual is their camouflage. After a long
march, supper cooked, night coming down,
the conversation passed around like a pipe,

one voice starts ambling down a path that forks
in unexpected directions and you feel
the great beast purring next to you in the dark,
its bristly chin on your shoulder, its breath in your ear.

AFTEREFFECTS OF BELL'S PALSY

Having a good and bad ear comes in handy.
My bad ear, victim of a surgeon's saw
screaming through bone to free a facial nerve,
has lost the very highest range of sounds —
bats, telephones, sirens at a distance,
mosquitoes if they're male, small children whining,
regret, ambition's wheedlings, most tactful hints.
Banshees can keen on my ridgepole all night long
and, exhausted, watch me leave for work,
brisk and refreshed from sleeping good ear down.

My undiminished left ear can perceive
the beginnings of nightmare in a sleeping child
two rooms away behind a closed door, hear
the click of covert glances at a party,
the first drop on the roof of the first rain
of April, surmise the maiden name and color
of the eyes of the grandmother of the boy
my daughter sits thinking of, based on her breathing.
It can hear loneliness seven lampposts down
the street, slamming like a screen door in the wind.

ODE TO MY BLADDER

Ideal travel companion,
faithful friend,
purse I smuggle
in my skeleton,
enchanted bag, expanding
contracting
to accommodate
whatever it is given.

Dependable
alarm clock,
little nag.

Interior moon,
always waxing, waning,
ruling never an
in-continent, but
an interior sea,
a predictable ebb and flow.

Hero and martyr
you once endured
eighteen hours,
Homeric, impossible,

in thrall to tour guides
and an utter absence
of facilities.

And blessed am I
among women, envy
of bullet-bladdered friends.
May I never
take you for granted,
corporeal donkey,
body's burro,
small porter
willing to carry more
and yet more,
hinting, grumbling,
yet never letting fall
your load.

Raised together, we know
one another's quirks,
are the same age,
and how I dread the day
you fail, faithful
servant, old family
retainer.

OUTSIDE INTERESTS

The scarlet birdhouse you gave me for Christmas
was, that first year, rewarded by a wren.
We braced binoculars, charmed to watch them wrestle
long straws sideways through that narrow doorway,
wondered how they accomplished anything,
so frequent was that bubbling, sudden song.

The next year a rose-breasted grosbeak
moved into the kitchen cupboard, behind the cans
of lima beans. Dinner was difficult,
but the sense of privilege compensated.

When the nesting pair of sandhill cranes
chose the living room sofa, we gave ground,
sitting on the bed to read the paper,
to eat our take-out, the barred owl on the bookshelf
asking "Who cooks for you?" New interests

drive out old. The cats left long ago.
Goldfinches scallop through the living room,
a lemon arpeggio in one window, out the other.
We tell ourselves the Canada geese are good
graphic design, if not quite furniture.

Listening for the field sparrow's decelerating
ping-pong ball, we turned the phone off. We
don't miss friends unwilling to debate
the relative thrills of hosting a white-throated
versus a chipping sparrow. They left
some time ago, murmuring about our loss
of habitat, their huge pale eyes turned inward.

LEARNING CURVES

Sam Clemens liked the hat, the glamour and dazzle
    of riverboat pilots. Charles Dickens saw
        in mastering shorthand the thin end of a wedge,

a crowbar to open his future. First you learn
    the alphabet, every point, bluff, broken-limbed
        cottonwood for twelve hundred twisted miles

and back. Then the arbitrary symbols:
    a thing like a cobweb signifies expectation,
        the tremendous effect of a curve in the wrong place,

the difference between a reef that's real
    and one that's wind on water. They look the same.
        You have to teach yourself to feel the difference.

Knowledge is no accessory, medal, hat
    you can take off. It eats at the crumbling banks
        of self, adds silt and snags to once bottomless channels.

The madness of having assumed an impossible task.
    And you have to know it backward, in the dark,
        as Bixby scolded Sam, even the bits you missed

by having to sleep, you have to be able to read it
    back and render it into English again
        by candlelight, galloping down a rutted road

with a deadline at its end, New Orleans, London,
    have to make Hat's Island by dark, must know
    a blot like a skyrocket stands for aspiration.

MOUNT ST. HELEN'S, MAY 18, 1980

Vancouver! Vancouver! This is it!

DAVID JOHNSON, VULCANOLOGIST

i

"They never found the body." Put five hundred
atom bombs in a mountain. Detonate
them sideways in what's called a lateral blast.
Park your trailer on that mountainside.
Be there when a Richter five-point-one
earthquake starts to build, the landscape slips.
You have five seconds. I don't think you have ten.
How will you spend your time?

ii

The vocabulary of catastrophe
is lovely, as if vulcanologists built
their laboratories out of slabs of jewels.
The words are handholds stapled to hurricanes,
full of *l*'s forcing the tongue to ululate:
Plinean column, pyroclastic flow,
blowdown, mudflow, steaming fumaroles.
Standing dead.

iii

I read it but I do not understand.
While the eruption lasted it says there was
a zone of silence sixty miles around

the mountain where nothing could be heard. Beyond
that zone, of course, they heard it from Saskatchewan
to Oregon—that part is big enough to grasp.
But a core of silence? I reread.

Koans, apparently, don't come with footnotes.
At the center of the whirlwind, the still, small voice.

iv

Enormous numbers cancel each other out.
Turn the telescope around. Condense your focus
to its finest gauge. Imagination
has better work to do than stretching huge
and thin. There's a word I've been trying to remember,
the word shouted by the young scientist
standing on the mountain when it blew,
the code that meant the moment had arrived. Two months of
waiting.
For two weeks that solid mountain bulged
sideways five feet a day and still stood firm.
There is a sequence of still photographs
but no film of the moment when it blew. There is
a tape, however, of David Johnson's voice,

saying that one word, repeating it,
shaking with excitement.

v

Looking for that word requires walking
knee deep in ash, eyes focused on the ground.
One side of your skull begins to bulge.
Find the word; your work has just begun.
Pick it up, wipe off the ash.
Maybe Heisenberg would understand—
if you witness this, you can't survive,
if you survive, you can't have witnessed it.
No amount of time would be enough
to cram this into words. It would not fit.
You must use code,
something you can't forget—
the word for home.
Your tone will do the rest.
Shout, "Vancouver! Vancouver! This is it!"
standing at ground zero of your joy.

SEXING THE ALLIGATOR

THE SWORD

Power is a sword in a ditch by the side of the road,
half buried in mud and dung, its ornate hilt
gleaming through last year's grasses and burdock leaves.

Say that a woman, on her way back from market, maybe,
load-light with coins in her pocket and headed for home
sees the gold glint and tugs till the whole length is loosened.
What then?

She'll make an odd sight dragging that thing beside her,
trying not to get muck on her market clothes. Many a man
would believe he was doing the right thing to wrestle it from her —
no business with such a thing, she could injure herself —
and stride off whistling while she rubbed her wrist.

But say that the day is late, the road deserted,
the lights from the windows beginning to glow in the yards
as she walks the last mile, switching her grip on the hilt
so the shaft runs straight down through her fist, a good walking stick,
its tip toothing into the roadway and pulling her on.

Think of the uses she'd find for it, getting it home,
such flexible metal, so strong and so sharp. It could be
lever and lightening rod, cleaver and chimney probe,

source of straight furrows for seeds in a small cottage garden
and brace to keep doors shut against the black fears of the night.

But hearing the echo in the back of her brain from her brothers,
"Women—they ruin good tools by using them wrong,
chisel for screwdriver . . ." being no fool, recognizing
the true nature of this tool, she keeps it hidden
so no one will be tempted to take it, learning
to get the good of it without cutting herself.

MARIAH EDUCATES THE SENSITIVE

In the first place,
you are not allergic to wool.
That lie is the bastard brat
of ignorance, overheating, and vanity.
You may be allergic to cats,
angora rabbits,
dust, mold, pollen, the stings of bees,
bad dreams, the semen
of Rh negative men,
or, if you were an ax murderer
in a former existence,
strawberries. You could be reacting
to chemical dyes, the sulfuric acid
they soak wool in to carbonize the hay,
sheep dip so deeply lethal
it kills on contact, bad vibes
from an old cryptorchid ram, hysteria,
or bad karma. But not wool.
Never wool.

Has it ever crossed your mind
that there are breeds,
that each breed extrudes
a different wool? You buy
a crappy, scratchy,

certainly Suffolk
sweater because you like
the pretty color,
then brag that you're too sensitive
to wear wool. What do you know
of Merino, Spanish wool so fine
it makes a grandmother's love
seem cold and harsh?
Men were beheaded
for smuggling these sheep.
You could spend a life
exploring the differences
between Icelandic and Churro,
Black Welsh Mountain,
Finn, Romney, Jacob, Corriedale,
Karakul, Cheviot, Shetland, Lincoln, Leister —
both Border and Blue Faced —
Coopworth, Cormo, Targhee, Wenslydale,
Herdwick, Swaledale,
Cotswold, God forbid,
Dorset, Tunis, Polworth, Rambouillet.
Then you could start on rare breeds.
Don't get me started.

Wool is the perfect fiber,
the only one
that insulates when wet.
Wet cotton, silk,
are out to save themselves, leaching
your body heat away.
Like us, wool breathes.
Unlike us, it's blessed with memory,
returns to its original shape when washed.

Wool is proof of a benign, personal God,
is grace, divine intervention at its best.
It's why sheep are mentioned in the Bible
more than any other animal.
I made that up,
but you believed me, proving
you've had your own suspicions
all along.

When mercury freezes,
hang your quilts on the wall.
Curl under wool.
Wool knows you're a mammal.
It's sympathetic, doesn't just conserve
body heat—it radiates it,
melting your bunched muscles
into something capable of sleep,
making sure your dreams
fill with green fields.

CROCHETING CHAOS

for Daina Tamina and Hinke Osinga

In America crochet's a racist subject.
     It's lower class, it's what the servants did,
the uneducated, factory girls,
     not to put too fine a point on it, the Irish —
heads bent over bits of bedspreads, doilies,
work spiraling outward.

Yet this Latvian mathematician owns a bowl
     of crocheted shapes she made to incarnate
what's been proved equations cannot prove —
     the hyperbolic plane in three dimensions,
curving away from itself at every point,
the opposite of a sphere.

(Incredibly, it's not just an abstraction;
     curly parsley, the rims of sea slugs show it.)
They look like brains, tree fungus, cauliflower.
     She's made a skirt to wear to conferences
with a crocheted hyperbolic hem.
Each of its ruffles ruffles.

Soviet bloc countries mass-produced
     shoddy products and educated women;
to be chic you had to make your own.

For the first time in history there were minds
containing both equations and crochet.
Daina Tamina's monitor

displayed a graph, smashed, butterflied and skewed;
    provable or not, she realized
the Lorenz Manifold's crochetable.
    Tall as a two year old, it models weather, winds,
predicts the movement of leaves in rocky streams,
a *chaotic attractor,*

which must be how those monks on Iona felt—
    sheep and silence, chaos rowing closer
(red beards, red flames) while they build, page by page,
    the Book of Kells—shapes curving around the words
like wind, like water, like the curl on the nape
of a girl crocheting a leaf.

They're illuminating—that is, making light.
    Holding darkness back, they tell the story
of that other case where what can not
be proved was once embodied.

CHILDREN IN CHURCH

are the white the artist adds,
the black,
to paint, producing tints and shades, amending
an otherwise too-pure pigment,
one without nuance or grit.
                                    They are at once
new-minted spirit, joy, small silver minnows
and absolute body, appetite, distraction,
the laundry after the rapture,
what you're given
to up the ante when it gets too easy.
Monastics should
import small children once a week the way
batters swing three bats,
runners wear ankle weights,
oysters inhale the catalyst of pearls.

BEADS

Because jewelry is useless, it indicates civilization.
It takes an hour to carve one ivory bead,
yet you can't eat beads, they won't keep you warm,
can't carry water, won't keep off the sun.
Beads are a leap. One bead alone is nothing.

I flatter myself I could have invented the pendant,
one shell or pierced stone hung between my breasts
on a length of grass or leather, although the braid
would be beyond me and I know my brain
could never have coughed up the knot. But beads.

They're tribal, reveal that nature once they're strung,
when, side by side, their differences become
less important than their mass, where they can
turn into something flexible and shining,
unified by an internal, invisible thread.

Of course the metaphor, the string, breaks down
before the beads—beads last. Which may explain
the ancient Russian grave they excavated,
two children laid skull to skull and strewn with beads,
with over ten thousand hand-carved ivory beads.

THE KALAMAZOO MASTODON

> The people of Kalamazoo have good gray souls.
> CARL SANDBURG

Nineteen twenty-seven, Patterson Street.
Clarence Miller feels his shovel hit a stone
too long, too heavy for him to lift alone.
John Clark comes over, cussing in the heat,
bends to wipe off dirt and mutters, "Sweet
mother of . . . that's not a rock, man. That's a bone."
When the professors finish, the count has grown
to skull, tusks, ribs—but no legs, and no feet.

It surprises us, raised on that refrain
about our good gray souls. Insults do stick
and we could be convinced that we're born mild
except that science hints we may contain,
just beneath our asphalt, below our brick,
something big and buried, something wild.

I'M IN LOVE WITH LEONARD WOOLF

his rectitude,
his long, thin face, his notorious horniness,   .
the palsy that trills his soup spoon on his plate
when he's underdressed among trivial people.
Oh, I'm in love with Leonard, but he thinks
I'm frivolous, not inhaling politics,
exhaling social programs.
So I've taken Virginia to Myrtle Beach.
I'm careful with her sunblock, and I make her
wear a gauzy ankle length pareo,
skimming the thin straps of her narrow sandals.
I buy her pastel drinks with umbrellas in them.
The karaoke was her own idea, though:
"Bus Stop," by the Hollies.
                    We stay six days,
then Leonard comes to get her, stiff in tweeds.
I hope the heat reminds him of the island
whose province he administered and loved,
and left for love and still must carry with him.
Her bronze shoulder blades embrace him; her wide hat
and huge sunglasses don't reveal her eyes.
She radiates well-being. A single drop
of sweat gleams in the shadow of his temple.

I'm watching to see if he'll reveal his lips.
I'm hoping for a handshake, the chance to feel
the tremor stress magnifies, Ceylon
in the palm of his hand.

IN ORDER TO SWALLOW, A FROG
HAS TO CLOSE ITS EYES

You really don't want to hear about the mechanics,
though you don't have much room to be haughty, sneezing
in traffic with the same side effect, no more choice.
We're passengers on the biology bus, reluctant
or willing, lucky to find a place to sit,
hoping not to be next to a runny-nosed
two-year-old who needs his diaper changed
or an old man carrying chickens upside down.
We think we want a seat alone by the window
even though what makes the trip worthwhile
may be the story the grandmother tells
loud enough for us to overhear,
the one where tongues of flame danced over every head
in the room where she preached, sang, conduit for Spirit.

Or it could be the sober ten-year-old
with the box lunch on his lap telling you
about the colt he saw born last spring,
the swift wet slide of limp mess managing
to stand, collapse, and stand. Oh, it is crowded
on this bus, no first class, no reservations,
there are smells and noise and something runs
over your foot and is gone too fast to see.
But in the darkest stretch of night, the quiet

like a light blanket over everyone,
you realize that for the last half hour
you've been holding a firm, warm hand, you feel the breath
of the approaching kiss and realize
you're glad and grateful not to have a choice.

NERUDA IN KALAMAZOO

Neruda shakes his head at Kalamazoo,
    but he's half-amused. There, in the corner
of Water Street Coffee Joint, in the flat cap,
    watching from under heavy lids with eyes
darker than the espresso he hasn't tasted.
    He's working on a metaphor equating
a nation's eros and its taste in coffee.

He isn't optimistic. Watching the slender,
    bundled young order their syrups, soy milk
(blood of anemic beans, he mutters), he worries
    for them. Such dilute fuel for love with all
those layers of wool, down, fleece to penetrate.
    He sighs. Even their pale eyes afford no traction,
strike no sparks. It's like wrestling water.

But as he shakes his head, he sniffs, looks up.
    Cinnamon. A girl at the counter is sprinkling
cinnamon straight into her coffee cup.
    The young man at the table to his left
forms a fist under the table. Outside
    the gravel is resolving into mud.
Well. Perhaps. He opens his paper, sips.

DEADHEADING WITH KELLEE

Kellee's telling me that she's in love.
We're snipping blossoms clobbered by the storm
that stomped through last night, downing power lines,
snapping branches, but freshening the ferns
we'd transplanted just that afternoon.

She starts by asking from behind the pots
on the far side of the patio,
"How do you decide how soon to use
the word *love*?" At first I think
she wants an answer, and I want to keep
her talking, to bask a little in her glow,
to siphon off a little carbonation
to my adult sludge, so I admit I wait,
coward, till the other says it first.
She agrees.
We're silent for a while,
the scrape of terra cotta pots on slate
as we rotate pots, the courting calls
of finches, chickadees, and red-winged blackbirds
the only sounds. Then, in the smallest voice,
"He said it." "Really?" "Actually," she says,
gathering momentum, "he said 'madly.'
'I'm madly in love with you.'"

Behind her in the woods a fallen tree
lifts the giant millwheel of its roots,
sunning the underside. Kellee plucks
sodden petals without counting loves me,
loves me not because she knows.

She goes on snipping off the spent, the bruised.
Plenty more buds where these came from. It's June.
I think she'd sing if only I weren't here.
The honeysuckle strangling the lilac
buys itself reprieve; it fills the air
with a perfume that's just not quite too much.

VALENTINE'S DAY IN KALAMAZOO

Cupid yawns and gropes for the remote.
This is Michigan, too cold for a gauze
jockstrap floating underneath this bloat.
Besides, bow season's over. Stretching jaws
around a belch, he shakes his head. The laws
against exposure make it tough — the cops
get Weather Channel backup here: "Because
exposed flesh freezes in ten minutes, tops,
be sure to bundle . . ." He smiles. Nothing stops
our boy. He lifts his clicker and that young
couple flares. Immediately she drops
her protests and her blouse, he finds his tongue.
Their skin learns that the best protective cover
is the equally exposed flesh of a lover.

TAKING JIMMY STEWART TO BED

Not *Rear Window*'s Stewart, who could resist
even someone as exquisite as Grace
Kelly, for God's sake, nor the one who kissed
Donna Reed's poor tantalizing face
with frenzied reluctance in the telephone scene
of *It's a Wonderful Life*. And certainly
not the Stewart of *Vertigo*, torn between
love and fear, tormented. No, I see
myself slowly unbuttoning the shirt
of Mr. Smith's innocence, certain I will be
the first to manage to move him from flirt
to frenzy, achieving the status instantly
of Wildest Moment. He likes it, I can tell;
he stammers afterward, "Gee, that was swell."

THE YEAR HITS PERIMENOPAUSE

Autumn has decided what the hell.
She knows the symptoms and already frost
has tarnished her. She's not a fool. She knows
however much she feels like May the snows
are coming, so before this chance is lost
she's going to wear red, show off her tits,
plump apples, bulge pumpkins. She is going to swell
each bunch of grapes to cleavage and shadowed musk.
Fuck decorum, honey, take a bite.
Take two. Each day is shorter than the last
and colder, so her unimpeachable night
is thick with glitter, rhinestones, sequins, glitz.
She thinks that maybe she'll even try her luck
and use her license for a few young bucks.

SOW'S EAR

I paid a fortune for this horrible yarn
    years ago, this overspun, thickthin mess,
this inferior string whose grubby lumps
    alternate with thin stretches kinked to thorns.
I was young. I was seduced by color
    and by funk, the way an ugly, confident man

makes conquests through persistence, the tang of revulsion.
    This is the Diego Rivera of yarns,
pop-eyed, pus-gutted. You could spin one better.
    So could the woman who sold me this, but she knows
bad sells "because it looks handspun," especially
    when she prices it high. This is cynical yarn.

For years I wouldn't knit with it. Disgusted
    with myself, I forgot it in a closet.
So coming across it by accident last week
    was bumping into Diego in Detroit;
after three children and years of happy marriage
    it would be silly not to have a drink,

to cast it on. My technique has improved,
    and as I watch the string and slubs form fabric,
as the plums, browns, blues slide through my hands,
    intriguing, compelling, I see there's no question
of stopping now. It won't take long to finish;
    I know I'm going to go all the way.

LILIUM ORIENTALE

Today I sided with the lilies. Not
Easter lilies, their cloying purity
too boring to violate. Not

Quaker daylilies, cheerfully surviving
drought and neglect to brighten July. And not
laboriously hybridized Asiatics

with names like 'Nutmegger' and 'Connecticut Yankee',
intruding indestructible burnt orange,
chrome yellow on June's semi-transparent charm.

Today I sided with Oriental lilies,
great recurving stars with thrusting stamens,
petals splashed with scarlet and burgundy.

Even the white ones revealing a handful of rubies
strewn across their smooth skin, indiscreet,
flaunting themselves like courtesans at high windows

allowing a handsome but impoverished student
a glimpse, their scent,
part cinnamon, part jasmine,

one that makes you open your mouth to breathe,
a smell that looks you right in the eye and smiles
while it slowly begins to unbutton its bodice.

HOW TO SEDUCE HENRY DAVID THOREAU

It would help if you could be a loon
or, more ethereal, the evening star
or the sound of a wooden flute at sunset.
Otherwise, it's going to take all summer.

Be more ethereal than the evening star
to begin with, then start coming closer,
otherwise it's going to take all summer.
Practice learning to walk like a doe.

Begin distant, then start coming closer
at evening, down there by the water's edge.
(Practice learning to walk like a doe.)
Don't look at him. Pretend he isn't there.

At evening, down there by the water's edge,
wearing your hair long and dressed in white,
not looking up, as if he weren't there,
remember that you mustn't say a word.

Of course your hair is long and you wear white.
Remember, he knows no girls, only maidens.
Silence helps him to seduce himself.
Celibates are irresistible.

Even knowing no girls, only maidens,
his high principles are still wrapped in flesh.
If you find celibates irresistible,
over a whole summer you might win.

His high principles are wrapped in flesh
and mystery might win, but ask yourself
why you find celibates irresistible.
I'm not that interested, but you should be.

Mystery might win, but ask yourself
why it would help if you could be a loon.
I'm not that interested, but you should be
the sound of a wooden flute at sunset.

TO A PICKY EATER AT LOVE'S TABLE

This isn't the love you sent back to the kitchen,
the one you now remember as seasoned exactly
to your taste, which you now admit you returned
because you weren't that hungry and because
you thought the kitchen would be open all night.

And now this is set before you. Ominous shapes
in — is it puttanesca? Hunan? — sauce
which stings the tip of your tongue. The smell that rises
repels, attracts — and is this pottery crude
or priceless art you're not qualified to judge?

You miss the pretty plate, that sweet, mild meal
that never burned your lips. I'm not saying make do.
I'm saying it's a long time between meals out here,
and gourmets are pressing their noses to the window
for a whiff of what is cooling on your plate.

AUGUST

Squirrels on the shed roof, trying to mate,
don't seem very good at it,
though the way he clasps
her approximate waist
with his almost arms,
seems nearly tender,
echoes the human. That,
and the way,
after several failed attempts,
they stand still, separate,
facing different ways,
for many minutes,
not touching,
not moving away.

LETTER TO MATT ON THE OPENING
DAY OF DEER SEASON

November fifteenth, but the air's warm as blood.
   I wear red, stick to paths through open fields,
      imagining you and your brothers in these woods.
A shot reverberates. Silence. Then another,
   companionable in this solitary day
      as laughter through a neighbor's distant window.

I know the warmth that lures me out to walk
   spoils your sport. You're wishing we had snow.
      I pictured you tracking pairs of dainty prints,

but no, you said it's easier to see
   blood on white, it's easier to follow
      and finish the wounded. You hunt by holding still.

Men free of women, women free of men.
   Your love's alone this weekend—for a moment
      you catch her city-girl scent. She's buying sheets—
three hundred thread count—sitting in coffee shops,
   having her nails painted red. Her eyes
      brown, luminous, are everywhere. Distraction.

In this late heat success is pressure. Cold,
    you could take your time, but by hunter's logic
    leisurely processing now risks everything
your patience won, risks having it turn bad.
    In weather like this the knives can't hesitate.
        In your haste milk washes blood from your hands.

STALLING

I'm teasing out this chickweed's single root,
loosing that green doily when the noise

I didn't realize that I was hearing
stops. I glance above the treeline, spot

the single engine Cessna, force myself
to inhale. They come out here to practice stalling,

to practice not to panic, learn to try
the next thing and the next thing and the next

till something works or till there is no next.
To "boston" is to pause when you are waltzing,

to vamp until the traffic of the dance
clears and you resume the swoop and turn.

Sleep apnea is almost never fatal.
His silence all last evening might not mean

treetops rushing up, branches smashing, boom
of fuel tanks bursting into blooms of flame.

Still, I let my breath out when I hear
the sky hum, toss the bright weed on the heap.

AMPLIFICATION

There's no need to be sentimental. Say the heart
    is a lamp burning whale oil or kerosene,
clean, bright enough for needlework or reading.
    Not feeble, not dim, but certainly domestic.

Outside the night bulges with dangers, both the prowling,
    predatory, coming-to-get-you kind
and the rooted, the lurking, the submerged
    waiting to rip the delicate bellies of boats.

And the heart, we've said, is a lamp. Then certain people,
    particular jigs of the pulse, some speeds of breathing
create around the heart a Fresnel lens,
    a system of prisms and mirrors twelve feet high

that reflects, refracts, and magnifies that lamp
    as it floats frictionless on quicksilver, turning,
dervish repeating, repeating a circuit of joy,
    its light now visible eighteen miles out to sea.

SEXING THE ALLIGATOR

A twenty-pound turkey takes longer to thaw than you'd think,
    than I thought.
At the sink, stuffing ready, I'm elbow-deep in carcass,
    grappling
with an inner handle, one end of the neck,
    shank set in ice.
It makes the bird seem turned half inside-out,
    like a casual sock.

The problem with alligators is even males
    go in an armored modesty,
as interior and private as their mates.
    So one naturalist
must grope inside, feeling for a penis
    or an absence
while at the other end a partner holds
    the jaws,
so weak to open, so strong to close.

My fingers freeze and burn. I'm running late.
    I've already thrown away the tidy packet

holding the limp liver, the white-wrapped kidneys,
    the small, tense nugget that is the heart.

THE GENOME FOR LUCK

Sidewalk ice so thin frost ferns its surface,
cat-ice. February sheathes claws to let us think
we might escape. It's toying with us. Wind
that bitch-slapped me last week today plays with my hair.
On bare twigs house finches are improvising riffs
no female finch with any sense will heed.
The bird that breeds now will hatch blizzard babies
that would die and take those fool genes with them.
Still, the angle of the sunlight prods,
the air is soft, and what if they were right,
what if this is anomaly, an odd
but permanent early spring? Maybe those fledglings
would survive, mate, and spread recessives for luck,
just the way others in my family tree
took the right boat, chose to leave Oklahoma,
went roller-skating a certain afternoon
in Detroit in nineteen forty-two
so that when I looked up, there you'd be.

LIDIAN EMERSON WATCHES HER HOUSE BURN, CONCORD, JULY 23, 1872

I am the calmest person here tonight.
From my best settee, bare feet in grass,
I watch one-armed Ephriam Bell up on the roof.
The smell of smoke blends with the scent of roses.

By the time we saw the thin, bright line
wavering in the dark, the fire had spread
from the garret down into the walls.
Fire at a distance sounds like rain.

Half the town is here. The men disguise
excitement with heroics, carrying
tables, flinging clothes from upstairs windows.
Someone else's shawl is on my shoulders.

Some fires burn themselves out. Caroline's letters
used to come for him by every post.
One has to choose. Not opening the door
to the attic gave us time to save the books.

Some things can't be saved. The parlor ceiling
is down, the floor's a lake, the yard a shambles,
heaps of clothes and books rise everywhere.
Maybe we should just have let it burn.

An attic fire thrives on inattention,
heat breeding in sealed rooms far from routine.
The light of flames through lathe was almost pretty,
the way enthusiasm can seem harmless.

The smell of smoke blends with the scent of roses.
Fire at a distance sounds like rain.
Someone else's shawl is on my shoulders.
Maybe we should just have let it burn.

PATTERN AND GROUND

CONSIDER HAIRS

Your nose and your ears keep growing as long as you live.
Think of it: Lilian Hellman forced to tote
that great zucchini, Auden's unfurling ears.
Cute is a survival mechanism;
consider harp seals, ask parents of two-year-olds.
So it's no wonder the carapace of age
frightens us; almost certainly we will not
develop sufficient charms to compensate.

Not for hairs, so often embarrassments.
These aren't the secret hairs of adolescence:
pubic disruptions, smooth armpits suddenly becoming
caverns dense with Spanish moss. Those shames
are secret. No, the hairs of age are public,
chins and moles for women, ears for men.
Eyebrows you could braid or bead.

                    But why
should only those hairs flourish that are unwanted?
If a wise providence chooses not to encourage
six brave hairs arching lonely from ear to ear
across the gleaming scalplands, well, all right.
But why couldn't the forces of disintegration
have evolved to encourage bourgeoning eyelashes, too?

Just as cheeks grow softer and softest, why
couldn't eyelashes come to resemble reeds
fringing still dark pools where lions drink,
grow heavy as Shetland ponies', as giraffes',
finally closing of their own soft weight.

EMERSON'S EYES

[Emerson] now got his own future exactly reversed when he
said, "You may perish out of your senses, but not out of your
memory or imagination."
ROBERT D. RICHARDSON

In the end, God cut Emerson a break.
That mind had been stoked nova-white for decades—
reading German philosophers, Hindu sacred texts,
to light the meadow where Waldo wrestled with
the angel of existence, demanding meaning.
No one's word was good enough for him.

And he lived. Any star can fill the sky
then fall in on itself, demanding darkness,   -
die of consumption, the Hellespont, the head
in an oven. He made his name then kept on living
up to himself, refusing to relax.
His first wife died at nineteen, coughing blood.
His first son died at five. Death circled him
like buzzards on a thermal. He persisted.

Finally God allowed that brain to slip
free from the limits of language, like
a watch spring from the constrictions of its case.
The ideas stayed; names went drifting off.
He started tying labels onto things:
an umbrella became "what the guest leaves behind."
Look at the final photos, the portrait on

The Portable Emerson. The brow is there,
the eagle's beak. Look closer, at the eyes.
As if through a backward telescope
you see the nebula that was his mind
spiraling dreamily out into darkness.

THE ONLY OTHER FEMALE IN THE HOUSE

She bought that foster son
a golden hamster
so he could practice loving.
It was nice not to be
the only female.

When Ginger finally
failed to reappear
she tried believing
she'd escaped with the mice

who would come in
under the sink but knew
that was also how
the black snake got in.

EGG TEMPERA PAINTING, KOO SCHADLER,
KALAMAZOO INSTITUTE OF ARTS

Turning, I saw a small painting, a turtle perched
on a speckled rock on a balcony rail,

draperies, a chamber behind, hills beyond,
and a bay or river. The turtle stands

almost tiptoe, chin raised. She'll like this,
I thought. I'll show her when she's well.

In the upper corner, a tall ship,
sails billowing full, is almost out of sight.

THE TUESDAY BEFORE OUR FRIDAY VISIT

She started to die
the night of the first
April rain.

AFTERTHOUGHT

She wrote love notes
in the steam
on the bathroom window.

After she died
when he took a shower
her handwriting appeared.

When he lost
the house too
he took the window.

MEETING EDWARD LEAR IN HEAVEN

She wears a retro dress,
the waist nipped small
now that the tumors
don't bulge, a skirt that swirls,
and dangling red earrings.

Time's different there
and just this second
she's spotted the tall man
excusing himself from Auden
and coming toward her, shy,
his hands outstretched.

ELEGY FROM HALFWAY UP THE DRIVE

First time this year. I'm idling up the drive,
foot off the gas, watching for hawks, for fawns,
wild turkeys—for the usual surprise,
swearing under my breath. First time without you.
The garden is just coming back to life.

I got the hours wrong for visitation,
arrived between rounds, everyone at dinner,
just you and me, and coming closer found
it was just me. I sat there with your shell.

I've never seen a turtle in the road,
ever. Sometimes by August I'll see them here,
dragging from pond to pond across the lawn
or digging up the drive to lay their eggs.
Never any other time.
                          But you
not only saw them everywhere, you'd stop
your car, get out, and haul them off the road,
your son slumped in an agony of cool.
You knew good deeds aren't easy, and you worried
about the one you found already hit,
shell cracked. Should you have left him in the road?
By moving him did you just prolong the pain?

They couldn't cure you. Once they'd lifted you
off the burning asphalt, set you down
in the cool, palliative grass along the verge
your son promised while you still could hear
always to pull those dummies off the road.

It rained last night. They'll need a load of gravel
sometime this summer. Just up ahead
there's something black down on the sandy path,
a tent worm nest, maybe, soaked and blown.
I slow my crawl to creep, come closer, brake.
A box turtle stands there, looking up.

I roll my window down, shift into Park.
We've got all day. I settle down to stare.

OUR THIRD WEDDING RECEPTION
THIS YEAR HITS ITS STRIDE

The floor's packed, partners optional. They play
"Down on the Corner," segue into "Shout";
we jump and hunker, our silk dignity out-
grown and molted. Now it's "YMCA."
This homosexual anthem has become
in the heavy hand of some god of irony,
the current wedding classic. The elderly,
the shy — this dance accommodates everyone,
like a favorite uncle, somehow still unmarried,
who flirts with great aunts, spins the flower girl,
waltzes gently with his fragile mother,
finds car keys, coaxes laughter from the harried
hostess, so the rest of us can clap and twirl
and briefly notice that we love each other.

PATTERN AND GROUND

All April I woke,
    far from home and lonesome,
to chickadees singing
    their "phoebe" courting call,
to robins flirting up
    then down the scale,
"cheerup," to house finches riffing.
    It took me two weeks to notice
I wasn't hearing the cardinal's
    "sweet, sweet, sweet."

It's a child's game,
    picking out what's different,
orange among apples,
    fried egg in a meadow.
"Which of these things
    does not belong"
they sing on *Sesame Street*.
    It's fun, even comforting—
we do love to exclude.

But in which lobe,
    what neural neighborhood,
do the truant officers lodge,
    the brain cells charged with noticing

absence, lack, the thing that isn't there
    but should be. "The dog did nothing
in the night." "That
    was the curious incident."
"Funny thing is,

there aren't any crops."
    The skipped heartbeat,
the failure to inhale;
    just when did she stop
laughing at your jokes?
No bogeyman can compete
    with how it feels
to turn from the elephants
    and find your mother gone.

I'm home now and the dawns
    are vehement with cardinals
singing the perimeter of my yard,
    the way I celebrated for a week,
singing praises to my coffee cup,
    my own pillow, husband,
praise even to the way the water tastes
    pouring from my home taps,
sweet, sweet, sweet.

WASHING MY HUSBAND'S KILT
HOSE: A 32-BAR REEL

You wash wool with shampoo. If you learn nothing
else today, learn that, to use shampoo
and water the temperature of a baby's bath.
What I have in the sink here aren't argyles,

but proper kilt hose I knit stitch by stitch, gray
for daytime, formal whites, choosing among
dozens of possible cuffs, customized gussets
to accommodate the bulging calves

of Scottish country dancers, whose heels must never
touch the floor, perpetual Barbie-feet
moving through jigs, reels, strathspays, till sweat and effort
equal ease and grace. The ones who say

"the important thing is just to have fun" miss
the most fun and the point, which is not fun
but joy, daughter of the difficult.
It's the kind of lesson climate teaches,

climates where sheer survival is success,
complaint as bad as cowardice, the humor deadpan,
self-control a given, not a goal —
an attitude empires find useful. Thermopolae, Dunkirk;

to delay catastrophe they place the best
regiments behind, the Spartans, Scots,
murdered or interned for the duration.
The Spartans combed and died. The Scots composed

a dance for captured warriors, "The Reel
of the 51st." Bemused Nazi guards
watched them practice, muscles taut as barbed wire.
It's hell to dance. These socks are stomped to felt,

dancing defiance of captors long since dead. No one
would knit these hose for any amount of money
a Scot would pay. Only one currency
is deep enough. I pat them out to dry.

To order or obtain more information on
these or other University of Nebraska Press
titles, visit www.nebraskapress.unl.edu.